Praise fo

This is the story of two real people who first met many years ago and felt a spark or connection, but could only dance at the very edge of love. A few years ago, the circumstances allowed them to create a complete loving connection and enjoy a passionate and enduring union. Then after such a short time, that connection was broken as one of them passed. Read how Diane was able to cope with such a cruel turn of events and turn her life from loss to a loving memory of her husband Bobby.

—Richard Barber, Frank Zappa's first tour manager

Bob Zappa was an amazing man. He lived a successful life which was in no way overshadowed by the achievements of his famed composer brother, Frank Zappa. When he met the equally amazing Diane Papalia, one thing was clear—they were soulmates and destined to be together. It took many years, but true love always wins. In this book, Diane reveals a story of love and loss, beautiful and heartbreaking, with surprises around every corner and a true and clear sense of joy. The Married Widow is a love story with a simple message: True love never dies.

—Scott Parker, host, ZappaCast: The Official
Frank Zappa Podcast

Diane Papalia has written a beautiful book about her marriage to Frank Zappa's brother, Bob. I was deeply moved by this book. It is a great companion piece with the two books Bob Zappa wrote, and I highly recommend it.

—Ed Palermo, The Ed Palermo Big Band

I first met Bobby in Lancaster, California, in 1955. We remained friends throughout the years until we met sadly for what would be the last time in 2018, where I found Bobby was still the same person I had met all those years ago. The Married Widow beautifully and poignantly describes the love that Bob and Diane found together.

—Denny Walley, guitarist, Mothers of Invention
and Captain Beefheart's Magic Band

Diane touched my heart so deeply with her love story. I'm sobbing right now though, and words seem so trivial compared to her raw emotion.

—Diann Peterson

Diane's love story is just charming and wonderful to read. She is a brilliant writer and has a great story. It is a bittersweet story, but isn't that a reflection of life? We could all do with a love story grounded in the real world.

—Harry Baer, MD

In this remarkable book, Diane provides us with a portal into her extraordinary relationship with Bob Zappa. At first seemingly implausible, and then at last inevitable, we are led through a labyrinth of joys and sorrows, lives lived and deaths endured, but always guided by an unbreakable thread of love. This is a must-read book of another kind.

—Ephraim Frankel, PhD, LMFT

Wow. Took my breath away.

—Bill Bielby, PhD, bassist and former president of The American Sociological Society

I got major chills and choked up reading about the details of Bob's passing and the afterlife occurrences. The sessions with (psychic medium) Drew Cali were amazing. Such a well-written human interest story of love, loss, and discovery of a new found reality.

—Carole Beebe

After reading this book, I'm sitting here smiling and crying at the same time. Your amazing memory and descriptions made me feel like I know "the man with the chocolate brown eyes." I just love that.

—Lana Rudner

It sounds like Diane and Bob were like trees growing together intertwined. Of course she still feels his presence. Lovely words. It's not a topic many people feel so comfortable talking about. I think this memoir will help a lot of people with their own grief.

—**Kilissa Cissoko**

The Married Widow is a moving love story that touched my heart. Diane and Bob used the time they had together well and found a way to stay close even when they could not be together physically. This story gives me hope in my own grief and bolsters my belief that love never dies.

—**Maria Leonard Olsen, author of** *50 after 50: Reframing the Next Chapter of Your Life*

THE
MARRIED WIDOW

MY JOURNEY WITH BOB ZAPPA

THE
MARRIED
WIDOW

MY JOURNEY WITH BOB ZAPPA

DIANE PAPALIA ZAPPA

**BOLD
STORY
PRESS**

Washington, DC

Bold Story Press, Washington, DC 20016
www.boldstorypress.com

First edition published June 2021

Printed in the United States of America
10 9 8 7 6 5 4 3 2 1

ISBN: 978-1-954805-02-6 (paperback)
ISBN: 978-1-954805-03-3 (e-book)

Library of Congress Control Number: 2021911606

Text and cover designer, Laurie Entringer; cover art, Hà
Nguyên; back cover photo, Maggie Yurachek Photography

This book is a memoir and it reflects the author's present
recollections of experiences over time.

The author requests your forbearance concerning the quality of
the photos in this memoir. She carefully selected a handful of
older photos to help illustrate her life with Bob Zappa, and family
members, and hopes you will enjoy the less-than-perfect images.

To my daughter, Anna V. Finlay,
with love and gratitude

And to my husband, Bob Zappa,
'til we meet again

CONTENTS

Contents

PROLOGUE

I met my husband, Charles Robert (Bob) Zappa, in 1986, but we were only able to be together after 2013. We married in 2015, and he sadly passed away in 2018. But those five years that we were together were the happiest of our lives. Once, at a dinner party I asked Ed Palermo, the pianist, to play the classic, "I Could Write a Book." And from across the room I sang to my husband:

And the simple secret of the plot
Is just to tell them that I love you a lot
Then the world discovers as my book ends
How to make two lovers of friends

This is that book, with our story.

CHAPTER 1

THE MAN WITH THE CHOCOLATE BROWN EYES

first saw Bob in January 1986, at a McGraw-Hill sales meeting in St. Louis. I was invited to that meeting to celebrate the success of the first edition of the college text, *Psychology*, by Diane E. Papalia and Sally Wendkos Olds, which was McGraw-Hill's "Book of the Year." Bob, its marketing manager, was "Marketing Manager of the Year." The book had sold 50,000 copies in its first year, which, in the world of college publishing, is pretty much unheard of. At the meeting, Bob was making a pitch to a group of sales representatives about a new book he was promoting. In college publishing, the marketing manager has to convince the sales force that it is worth their time to try to get a book adopted by professors who teach the relevant course. Bonuses depend on it.

Bob was a compelling speaker, very funny, and I found him adorable. He was definitely "my type"— not too tall or too short, dark complexion, chocolate brown eyes, a sexy Italian man. I was standing because it was a full house. I remember the people— editors, sales reps, marketers, and other corporate types—around me saying, "You know who that is? That's Frank Zappa's brother."

The meeting in St. Louis was a blast. I closed down the hospitality room every night. This was a partying crowd, even after a full day of learning about McGraw-Hill's new titles. The food was great and the drinks flowed endlessly. But Bob, being a bit more prudent, avoided the hospitality suite and went to bed early.

A second sales meeting was held that January at the Nassau Inn in the beautiful college town of

Princeton, New Jersey. When I was first invited to that meeting I declined, saying I had to be at work and couldn't attend. I was a tenured full professor of Child and Family Studies at the University of Wisconsin-Madison, teaching undergrads and grad students. The meeting in St. Louis had been held before second semester began so I went guilt free. But recalling that I had had such a good time in St. Louis, I decided to go to the second meeting, and arranged for a TA to teach my classes in Madison.

The man with the chocolate brown eyes. (Photo by author.)

It was a decision that would change my life.

Bob was assigned the task of collecting me at Newark airport and getting me to Princeton. He met my flight, took my floral brocade bag, and we headed for the parking lot. I remember his rental car was white and I wore a hot pink coat. When we got in the car to drive to Princeton, he took a wrong turn leaving the airport. The ride, plus the wrong turn, took an hour or so. We spoke easily together, about so many things— my books, his brother Frank, publishing in general, and McGraw-Hill in particular. I learned he had been married for 21 years and had a 15-year-old son. I told him I had been married for 10 years, but I had no children at the time. His wife, Marcia, was a nurse. My husband, Jon, was a pediatric oncologist.

Both nights that I was in Princeton, I had dinner with Bob along with a crowd of editors, sales reps, and marketers. The first night was a banquet and, when he saw there was only one other person at my table, he came over and sat next to me. The next night, dinner was with a small group that went to a local restaurant. Bob and I sat together at the end of a long table, lost in our own little world. He sat to my right. I found out he was 42; I was 38.

When we talked later about that dinner, we both remembered an intense and immediate connection. Looking back, we realized that's when we fell in love.

CHAPTER 2

BREAKFAST AT WOLF'S DELI

After that fateful meeting in Princeton, I boarded a plane in Newark for the trip home to Madison. I don't remember too much about that trip except I went back to the airport by car service since Bob was tied up with more sales meetings.

When I got back to Madison, I was back to life as usual. Except life really wasn't "usual." I felt a need to stay in touch with Bob, and on some level, wanted to know him better, and to have him in my life. My world had shifted in a way that would affect both of us forever.

I had been on the faculty in Madison since 1971, right after getting my PhD in developmental psychology from West Virginia University. The semester when I met Bob, I was teaching a couple of classes including a huge undergraduate course on human development. There were about 600 students gathered in a large auditorium. I took a "sage on the stage" approach in which I talked and they listened. Or at least that was the idea. At the same time, I was teaching a graduate seminar on adult development and aging.

I also worked with a small group of very bright and very eager graduate students who wanted to do research about how to stay sharp cognitively as you got older. UW was a "publish or perish" world, and I quickly learned how to play that game. Besides my teaching and research, I was working on revising my three college textbooks. I figured that I would see Bob two or three times a year when I ventured to the Mc-Graw-Hill corporate headquarters in New York City to report on how my projects were coming along. It wasn't much, but at least I had something to hold on to. Or so I thought.

Then, one day a few weeks after the sales meeting in Princeton, I got a call from my editor. She told me Bob was leaving the College Division of McGraw-Hill and had accepted a position as General Manager of Datapro Research Corporation, a subsidiary of Mc-Graw-Hill, located in Delran, New Jersey, about 15 miles from Philadelphia. Datapro produced print publications on data processing. One of Bob's additional responsibilities was to set up a Datapro office in Lausanne, Switzerland. These new responsibilities came with a big salary increase and, eventually, promotion to Vice President. He told me later he felt that he had no choice but to take it. So he split his time between Delran during the week, home in Ridgewood, New Jersey, on weekends, and Lausanne often for a couple weeks at a time.

When my editor told me this, I was stunned. Devastated, really, because my "plan" to see him a few times a year was ruined. But I decided that I had to see him one more time. I tracked down his phone number at McGraw-Hill, and made up some question only he could answer. It was lame, I knew, but desperate times call for desperate measures.

During that call to Bob, I mentioned that I would be coming to the city soon and hoped I could take him to breakfast to celebrate his career move. He agreed, so we set a date and time at the beginning of February when I would be staying at The Pierre, an elegant hotel on 5th Avenue, across from Central Park. I wanted to take him there for breakfast, but he told me The Pierre was too rich for his blood. So instead we headed over to Wolf's Deli on West 57th Street. I remember he had oatmeal (it was, after all, February) and some sort of egg dish. I had coffee. Black, and plenty of it.

And so there we were at Wolf's over breakfast, realizing that the connection was still there. We both knew that we wanted to get to know each other better. We agreed to keep in touch. And so we did.

CHAPTER 3

MOVING TO PHILADELPHIA

Bob left McGraw-Hill and New York City in February, a month after we had first met. He began his job at Datapro that same month, often staying in a motel in Delran, but he also traveled to Switzerland every few weeks.

One of his main responsibilities was to set up the Datapro outpost in Lausanne. He had to find office space, hire personnel, make sure furniture and other supplies were on hand, and generally establish and then ensure that the office ran smoothly. To do this, he spent many weeks there. He told me that at least he got to fly business class, stay in five-star hotels, and enjoy gourmet meals. And Lausanne was a gorgeous city on the edge of Lake Geneva. But the frequent travel to Lausanne—and because he needed to spend weekdays in Delran when he wasn't in Switzerland—meant that he spent a lot of time away from his adolescent son, and he felt guilty about that. He told me later that this was one of the biggest regrets of his life.

After our breakfast at Wolf's, we wrote to each other often. His letters via the US Postal Service, not email, were always newsy, and very, very funny. When he was in Delran, we had many long, intimate phone calls. We never, in all our time together, seemed to run out of things to say.

Around the same time, in early 1986, another change was in the air. My husband Jon was being recruited by Children's Hospital of Philadelphia, known as CHOP, for a position in the Pediatric Oncology Department. CHOP was and still is one of the best children's hospitals in the country, so it was a definite step up from the University of Wisconsin Department of Pediatrics where Jon was on the faculty.

Of course, I was all for it. My parents, both in their 70's, lived in Fort Lee, New Jersey, about 100 miles from Philadelphia. And, I would also be closer to Bob. As much as I loved Madison, a beautiful college town on four lakes where I'd lived since 1971, moving East was moving home.

The recruitment process at CHOP was lengthy, so it wasn't until September 1987 that Jon's work there was set to begin. So I resigned from my full professorship in Madison at the ripe old age of 40, sold the house, packed up our belongings, and never looked back.

Before the actual move, I had made several trips to Philadelphia to check out places to live. I loved the bustle of city life and I thought center city would be a good spot. But by that time we had a one-year-old daughter, Anna, so we settled on a house in suburban, bucolic, and totally boring Haverford, on Philadelphia's ritzy Main Line. There I spent my days revising my books and hating the suburbs.

But at least there was a letter from Bob waiting in the mailbox when I moved in. Bob and I saw each other only three times after I moved to Pennsylvania but we talked on the phone almost every day. He even came over for dinner one night when Jon was away. I remember making linguine with oil and garlic, anchovies, and capers—the way to that Italian guy's heart.

Two years later in February 1988 Bob lost his job at Datapro, a victim of corporate restructuring. So he went back to New York and eventually landed a job as a vice president at Macmillan. But not without our first kiss finally happening after the dinner I'd prepared, right there in Haverford, almost two years after we had first met. It was passionate and sensuous, a promise of greater times to come . . .

CHAPTER 4

MOVING TO THE BIG APPLE

After about a year in Pennsylvania in 1988, Jon was invited to interview for the position of Vice Chairman of Pediatrics at Memorial Sloan-Kettering Cancer Center (MSKCC). Landing a job at Sloan-Kettering, one of the premier centers for cancer treatment and research in the country, was an even bigger step up than Children's Hospital of Philadelphia, and the process was somewhat more involved. There were many rounds of interviews and reference checks. The Chairman of Pediatrics even interviewed me to determine whether I would be willing to move to New York. He seemed relieved when I said I'd love to. He told me later that it was difficult to recruit good people because the cost of living in the city was sky-high and the crime rate even higher. It was often the spouse who put the kibosh on moving to New York.

Ever since I was a child I wanted to live in Manhattan. My family's home while I was growing up was in the Palisades section of Fort Lee, an upscale part of town. I could see New York City from my bedroom. We were close enough to watch the cars on the George Washington Bridge. I'd often ask my dad, a lawyer in Englewood, New Jersey, why we weren't living over there rather than just looking at it. But he hated the city—the dirt, the noise, the crime, and the crowds. He just didn't appreciate the place at all! But I did, and I was thrilled to be moving there.

Before Jon and I left Philadelphia, I made a number of trips to the city, either to go to McGraw-Hill on business or to look for a place to live. When I had a meeting or event at McGraw-Hill, Bob and I would catch up in the late afternoon. We would often meet at Hurley's Saloon on West 48th Street, where the Mc-Graw-Hill crowd would go after work. Hurley's has been around since 1892 and has a classic New York City vibe. It's a great place to have a drink or two before heading on to dinner, or the theater, or even back to the suburbs. It's one of those places that defines New York City. Bob told me later that he loved when he'd spy me from his window seat at Hurley's, dashing across the street and into his arms. Often, after Hurley's, we'd go to JR's for dinner—a casual, dimly lit little place near my hotel that served traditional bar food. It was over cheeseburgers and fries there that I told Bob I was in love with him. And then he looked into my eyes and said that he loved me, too.

After many train rides between Philadelphia and Penn Station, I finally found a place for my family to live. It was a three bedroom in a high-rise apartment on East 72nd Street called River Terrace. The doormen wore white gloves, the service was impeccable, and we had a view of the Empire State Building and the Roosevelt Island tram. Sotheby's was on the corner. There were benches at the end of the street where you could sit and watch the barges and tug boats on the East River. Plus Jon could walk to work from this apartment.

So, in September 1989, Jon, our three-year-old daughter Anna, her nanny Mary, and I moved to New York City. I felt that I was home at last.

Once I got to New York, my relationship with Bob deepened. We couldn't see each other often, but we talked on the phone almost every day. We felt that we were arriving at a point where a decision had to be made about our being together. But we both had responsibilities to our families and careers, and those won out, at least for a while. So, despite the fact that we were finally in the same place at the same time, we agreed that we needed to take a break.

CHAPTER 5

THE APRIL FOOL

Even without my almost daily phone calls with Bob, I enjoyed New York City life. I loved the museums, the restaurants, the theater, and the hustle and bustle of the city that never sleeps. Anna was in school; I was making new friends and still revising my textbooks. Both Jon and I were foodies and sometimes we'd hit two restaurants on the same night. It had been four years since Bob and I had agreed that we'd focus on our families, but I still couldn't get the sexy Italian guy with the chocolate brown eyes out of my mind.

On December 4, 1993, I saw a front-page article in the *Times* that Bob's brother Frank had died after a long battle with prostate cancer. I knew how close Frank and Bob had been, especially when they were kids, so I picked up the phone to call Bob and offered my condolences. We talked for quite a while and all the old feelings bubbled right up to the surface—for both of us. We started a routine of calling periodically and eventually went back to almost daily phone calls. We also saw each other once in a while, and those times only brought us closer together physically and emotionally.

Meanwhile, my relationship with Jon was getting more and more rocky. We simply were very different people. He was career driven and competitive. While I was equally successful, my career wasn't my essence. And if I thought the pressure to succeed had been intense at Children's Hospital of Philadelphia, it was much more so at Sloan-Kettering. And Jon worked incredibly long hours that cut into our family life.

Bob was so different from Jon. While Jon believed that you live to work, Bob believed that you work to live. Bob was modest, and I found that refreshing. And his sense of humor was dark and his wit razor sharp. We both loved to laugh and were good at bringing that out in each other. We were a good match—clearly a better match than Jon and I. I just wasn't sure what to do about it. However, one of the pieces was about to fall into place.

On a sunny Friday in November 1997, Jon put 11-year-old Anna on the school bus to take her to The Hewitt School, a private girls' school on Manhattan's Upper East Side. When he came back inside, he told me bluntly, "I don't love you and I want a divorce." I watched him pack some clothes and take off. Divorce was a messy, miserable process, but after much wrangling, we were finally free of each other early in 1999.

In 2001 I bought a cottage in Newport, Rhode Island. Newport is a great little city, full of history, culture, vintage homes, renowned music festivals, and good restaurants. I loved its location by the water. My cottage, built in 1745, was my dream home. I still was living primarily in New York, but Newport was my summer place. Throughout this time, Bob and I continued our frequent phone calls. We would see each other in New York when we could. By this time, Bob was working at Oceana Publications, a small company in Dobbs Ferry, New York, about 20 miles from Manhattan and still lived with his wife, Marcia, in Ridgewood, New Jersey. When he could, Bob would take the train into the city to see me. Sometimes he would come to my house, but other times I would meet him at Grand Central, where we'd maybe grab lunch and a drink, or just walk around the city, happy to be with each other.

But we discussed our relationship, and Bob finally acknowledged that we needed to be together. So, in late March 2001 he left his wife Marcia. At first he stayed in a hotel near his home for several days, and then we decided to meet at my cottage in Newport. My daughter was still young, and I would not have been comfortable having him stay with us in New York. So Bob and I spent three magical days together in Newport. We made dinner and danced in the light of a fire Bob made in the fireplace. We explored Newport together, and dined at a romantic Italian restaurant in town. We even spent time on line looking at New Jersey real estate that we might consider for our life together. At the end of the weekend, he drove me back to my home, and kissed me goodbye.

But as I later learned, Marcia refused to give up on their marriage, and she knew how to pressure him to stay. She said that if he didn't return, she would tell their son why Bob had left. There was nothing more convincing that she could have done; Bob's guilt and concern about his son was overwhelming.

So, after our too-brief weekend together in Newport, Bob had quietly decided that he had to return home to his wife. That was April 1, 2001.

April Fools Day . . .

CHAPTER 6

THE BREAKUP
AND BEYOND

When it dawned on me that Bob had returned to be with Marcia after our weekend in Newport, I was devastated. He wouldn't talk to me on the phone, and he changed his email address. I tried to contact him, but I couldn't find a way. Maybe I should have known better than to let myself get so fully involved, and to have believed that Bob was ready to leave his family. But I did believe him and I trusted him. It all seemed pretty straightforward to me—we loved each other, and we wanted to be together.

However, when we finally got together in 2013, I realized he simply felt that he had no choice but to leave me. He took his obligations and commitments more seriously than his own happiness. And, at the age of 21, he had made that commitment to Marcia.

The year 2001 was a difficult one for me as I tried to regain my equilibrium. At that point Anna and I were living in the townhouse that Jon and I had bought on East 18th Street. It was a beautiful place, four stories and a tranquil garden off the kitchen. I used to love sitting in that garden, having meals there as soon as the weather was good, or just reading and catching some sun. If I listened carefully, I could hear the next-door neighbors in their garden, chatting, laughing, and eating, too.

The house had a small basement room and bath where my friend, Jeffrey, lived. Jeffrey was a professional pianist, whom Jon, Anna, and I had met in Positano, Italy, in June of 1994. Jeffrey had been living in New York City's Chelsea neighborhood, but he snagged a two-month gig playing piano in Positano at the hotel where we were staying. Le Sireneuse is a luxurious hotel in the heart of that city. We took meals on its outdoor patio overlooking the sea, where Jeffrey played a white grand piano. Positano, a hilly village on the Amalfi Coast, is a breathtakingly beautiful place. And the trip to Italy was meaningful for me as I visited for the first and only time the land where my ancestors came from.

Jon and I hit it off right away with Jeffrey, and when we realized he lived near us in the city, we got together and became fast friends. In early 1997, Jon and I invited him to move into that basement room. After my divorce from Jon, Jeffrey stayed in the townhouse until I sold it in 2004. He had a room in Newport, too. He was one of a few "angels" who helped me through the breakup with Bob. When he saw I was down, he would ask me what Broadway musical I wanted to hear and he'd sit down at the piano and play for me. That, and a few glasses of wine, actually helped.

After Anna finished her freshman year at York Prep, a private coed school in the Upper West Side of Manhattan, Jeffrey, Anna, and I headed back to Newport. Once I got there, a month or two after Bob left, my friend Sue flew in from Madison to Providence, Rhode Island, where she rented a car, drove to Newport, and took care of me. She dragged me to go shopping, to restaurants, and to sit by beautiful Narragansett Bay. She tried anything to get me out of my funk. And that helped, too. I ended up having a pretty good time in Newport that summer, and for the next couple summers as well.

"It is what it is!" I thought about Bob's decision to leave. "And what it is with Bob is 'over'."

Except it wasn't.

CHAPTER 7

MOVING TO THE WEST SIDE

ate in 2004 I put the townhouse on East 18th Street on the market. It was too big, and was quickly turning into a money pit. It seemed like everything was breaking down all at once. The ConEd bills to heat or cool the place were out of sight. And dealing with strict city regulations regarding snow removal, garbage collection, and recycling was becoming overwhelming. The house eventually sold, fortunately, and for over three times what Jon and I paid for it in 1995.

After the sale, I needed to find a place to live and decided to take a look on the Upper West Side. I really liked that area when Anna went to school there, and I was delighted to find a condo/duplex apartment at a price I could manage at The Level Club on West 73rd Street. The Level Club is a full-service prewar building with a wonderful live-in super, and a great staff. I loved the new apartment, and I really loved not having to do much of anything to maintain it. Anna and I moved there in late 2004. There wasn't a room for Jeffrey in my new place, so he decided to return to Montgomery County in Pennsylvania to be near his family. But Jeffrey visited often, and we enjoyed each other's company until his untimely death from lung cancer in 2007. He was only 54 years old and my best friend. His passing away broke my heart; I still think of him often with fondness.

As much as I loved my cottage in Newport, I was using it less and less, so in 2004 I sold it, too. My apartment at The Level Club was small and Anna really wanted to branch out, so I took my profit from the

Newport sale, and got a place for her in a condo in Hell's Kitchen, about a mile from me, where she lives till this day!

My life had fallen into a happy routine. I had a group of friends to spend time with, and I was enjoying the new life I'd created. But then one day early in 2005, four years after he had returned to his wife, the phone rang. Bob had tracked down my new phone number and said he wanted to ask me something. If I recall, I think it was about a book he had started to write about his shared childhood with his brother, Frank. So it seemed he was pretty good at finding a lame excuse to call. Just like me.

During our conversation, he told me that our breakup was hard on him, too. So hard, in fact, that shortly after it, he had a verbal dust up with his boss at Oceana, who fired him on the spot. So, at the age of 58 Bob had to find a new position in publishing or start a whole new career. He chose the latter and applied to become a New York City teaching fellow. That program was designed to recruit potential teachers, many of them making a midlife career change, to staff schools in high-risk areas in New York City. It was almost as hard to get into as Harvard, but Bob made the cut and through that program got his Master of Arts in Education from Lehman College in 2005.

After that call, Bob and I easily and automatically fell back into our old routine. We spoke on the phone once or twice a day, and we emailed frequently. He told me he still loved me and wanted to be together. And I told him I loved him. But again, Bob just couldn't make the break from his family. So, in early 2006, our renewed connection was over. Again. And this time I thought for real.

Of course, this breakup hurt, but at least I had had enough common sense not to see him during this time, even though he wanted very badly to see me. I wanted no more physical intimacy with him.

But sometimes an emotional affair is the hardest to get over.

CHAPTER 8

THE LETTER

Something felt different about 2013. From very early that year I was a bit "on edge," feeling like my world was about to shift again. Even my friends noticed a change.

I remember getting the mail on Monday, August 19. It was mostly the usual assortment of catalogs, bills, and junk. But at the bottom of the pile was a plain white envelope. My name and address were typed, but there was no return address. I figured it was more junk, and I almost didn't open it. But when I did I exclaimed to the friend who was with me, "It's from Bob!" It had been seven years since I'd last heard from him. This is, in part, what he wrote:

> "Dear Diane,
> I've been trying to write this letter to you for a very long time. I simply want to apologize for all the pain and heartache I've caused and hope that you have found comfort and happiness with someone who is caring and more deserving of your love. I know it comes far too late to have much meaning, but it's the best I could do."

He then went on to say that Marcia had passed away in June of pancreatic cancer. So now I understood what that "different" feeling was all about.

I wrote back immediately, sending him a card saying, "I still love you and always will. I am alone."

On August 23, he emailed me saying, "I got your card and was surprised by your comment. I can only think of how much I have screwed things up, and I certainly do not deserve your forgiveness, let alone your love . . . I often think of you and the moments we shared . . . and I find comfort in those times. Diane, I would like to see you again. I don't know what you feel about that but whatever you decide, I will accept. Love, Bob."

I emailed him back and said we needed to talk first, so we had a lengthy phone call the next day. It was the first of many before I actually agreed to see him. I remember one phone call vividly when he asked, "Diane, could you see me as your husband? And I said, "Yes, do you see me as your wife? "All the time," he replied.

Bob kept pressing to get together so I finally suggested New Year's Eve. I liked the symbolism of a new year and a new beginning. He didn't much care for that. So we decided to finally see each other on Saturday, October 19. He came to my apartment for the weekend, and all the pieces fell into place. That easy comfortable intimacy we always had had survived our long separation. I couldn't believe I was kissing him, holding him, loving him. It was what was meant to be. He told me later when he first saw me he thought, "This is the woman I love, and I'm going to make this right."

On October 22, I wrote to him, "I still look at our affair with some guilt and shame, but I guess we were two souls who found and needed each other and in struggling to play that out, we broke a few rules. I don't take that lightly but I'm starting to understand what happened." And Bob replied, "Things happened that shouldn't have . . . but they did. We're not the first couple to go through this but at least I did the best for

Marcia during a difficult time for her. And throughout it all you stood by me. We have nothing to be ashamed about because our lives have finally intersected and we are headed into the future together . . . I'm moving forward with you, and that is all that matters."

The next time we got together was October 31, 2013. That time he got down on one knee and asked me to marry him. "Of course," I murmured as he placed a diamond engagement ring on my trembling hand. Finally, after 27 years, we were going to get where we'd always wanted to be.

Bob had just turned 70 and I was 66.

CHAPTER 9

BOBBY'S BACKSTORY

Bob was born in Baltimore, Maryland, on August 29, 1943, the second of four children. His father, Francis Zappa, was born in Partinico, Sicily, in 1906. Bob's mother, Rose Marie Colimore, was born in Baltimore in 1912, and had Neapolitan roots. The family structure was very traditionally Italian. Dad made the decisions and everyone else fell into line. Bob described his mother as "a quiet woman, a good cook, and a wonderful mother" to Frank, Bobby, Carl, and Candy. He described his father as "authoritarian and stubborn."

The family eventually moved from Baltimore to Edgewood, Maryland when his father got a job at the chemical weapons section of the Aberdeen Proving Ground in Edgewood. But in 1951, when Bob was eight, his father took a job at the Naval Post Graduate School in Monterey, California, a quaint seaside town about 100 miles south of San Francisco. The family piled into the Henry J, a cheaply made car that Bob described as the Yugo of its day for the drive across country. His father promised them a journey full of great adventures, but Bob recalled it as a long, torturous trip on Route 66.

When the Zappa family first saw the sheer beauty of California, though, they were hopeful that the move west might have been a good idea after all. But a series of job changes for his dad took their toll. In his memoir *Growing Up Zappa*, Bob described how on Saturdays his father would take him and Frank to nearby Castroville ("the artichoke capital of the world"). There they would follow trucks loaded with

The entire Zappa clan, taken in 1953 in Claremont, CA. Back row: Dad, Frank, Bobby, and Mom. Front row: Carl and Candy. (Photo courtesy of Patrice (Candy) Zappa-Porter's personal collection and used with her permission.)

artichokes and collect the ones that had fallen off the trucks onto the road. Bob said that his father told them that the freebies tasted better. At first, he said, it seemed like the coolest thing they could do on a Saturday morning. After a while, though, it began to sink in that they were picking up fallen artichokes because they were poor. Bob observed that his father was trying to make a game out of something that was actually a necessity.

Bob's family moved at least seven times in California. Each time the family was uprooted, forcing the siblings to make new friends and adapt to new schools. Bob was told these job changes were his dad's attempt to provide a better life for his family. But looking back, Bob wondered if his father's difficult personality may have been the real reason behind those moves.

Bob's parents did not encourage him and his education. They didn't even bother to check if he'd done his homework. His father was convinced that Bob would never make anything of himself and he never missed a chance to tell him so.

In 1961 Bob was about to graduate from Claremont High School. While his peers were applying to college, Bob didn't know what to do next. And then, one day when Bob was 17, his father told him he'd taken yet another job, this time teaching in Florida. Bob dreaded the prospect of another move, this one across the country, when his father asked him, "And what are your plans?" It took a moment for Bob to realize that he was being left on his own, alone. He was disoriented, then angry, panicked at the thought of being homeless. Even as an adult, he still recalled the trauma of this moment.

During Bob's senior year in high school, he had joined a scout troop. There he met Norm Hines, the troop leader and a senior at Pomona College. When Norm heard of Bob's predicament, Norm and his new wife, Anne, invited Bob to live with them. Bob wrote, "I was yearning for a shred of security, anything that would keep me on course and provide stability." So he gratefully accepted their offer.

Bob was grateful to Norm and Anne Hines for taking him in, but he knew he couldn't stay there for long. Three months at Cal Poly Pomona convinced him that college was not for him, at least not in 1961. So he decided to look into the military. A Marine Corps Staff Sergeant was his first point of contact and he told Bob that if he enlisted, the recruiter would personally recommend him for Sea School, an elite group of Marines that guarded American embassies in exotic places. So Bob signed on and endured Basic Training in San Diego. But Sea School did not work out as the recruiter had described, and Bob felt betrayed. However, he did get to see some "exotic places." First, he participated in setting up the blockade around Cuba during the Cuban Missile Crisis of 1962. After three months aboard ship sailing around Cuba, the crisis ended. For the next 15 months, Bob was deployed to Okinawa for further training, and then went on to Vietnam. When Bob returned home to California late in 1964, Frank was there to greet him, just as Frank had done when Bob graduated from Basic Training. Bob's parents did not show up for either occasion.

As tough as it was, Bob found that the Marines provided the much-needed structure and sense of belonging to something bigger that he craved. He would like to say, "Once a Marine, always a Marine." It made him proud.

Once out of the Marines, Bob and another Marine friend, Gery Gomez, the son of baseball legend, Lefty

Gomez, moved into an apartment in Pomona, California. Bob applied for reinstatement at Cal Poly and was admitted, earning a Bachelor's degree in history and political science in 1969.

Bob had been introduced to Marcia, a psych nurse in San Diego, in October 1964. Their courtship was brief; four short months later they married in January 1965, and had one child, their son Jason, in 1971. The marriage and his child provided Bob with the same sense of structure and security that he craved, a dominant need for Bob throughout his life. Their marriage was rocky, and he stuck it out. They had been married for 48 years when she passed away in 2013.

Early in their marriage, Bob worked for a janitorial service and as a bill collector. But with a baby on the way, he knew it was time to find a job that at least had health benefits. Through networking with a former college professor, Bob was introduced to a field sales representative for McGraw-Hill, one of the biggest college textbook publishers in the world. A rep's job was to talk to college professors about the textbooks McGraw-Hill had published, and to convince them to adopt those books. Bob was very interested in the position because it came with benefits, a company car, an expense account, and two months off in the summer. After a series of interviews, he was offered the San Bernardino sales territory. There was a lot of material to master, but Bob landed a few significant book adoptions, so he came to the attention of the corporate offices in New York City. There the position of Physics Editor had opened, and Bob was invited to interview. So, in July 1975, he flew to New York City. He was offered—and accepted—the job on the spot.

Bob and his family relocated to Ridgewood, New Jersey the next month and Bob began the weekday commute into the city. Once Bob settled in, he excelled in this position and was promoted to other positions at McGraw-Hill as well. One of these was Senior Marketing Manager, the position he held when we met in 1986.

After Bob left Datapro in 1988, he was Vice President at Macmillan until 1990. From there he went to Thompson Professional Publishing until 1994, Simon & Schuster until 1996, and Primedia until 1999. His last position in publishing was as Vice-President of Marketing at Oceana Publications from 1999 until 2001.

Bob began teaching in 2002. His first assignment was in a middle school in the Sound View, a low-income section of the Bronx, with challenging students who often resorted to physical fights. He taught US history to seventh graders in summer school. He was assigned to work with an experienced teacher and, when that teacher retired in two years in 2004, Bob was supposed to take his place. At the same time, he was working on his Masters degree, so he was essentially a student teacher at the age of 58! But Bob was a survivor and he did what he needed to do.

Ultimately the teacher Bob was to replace in 2004 decided not to retire after all. So Bob's next job was teaching US history and economics at The School for Excellence, also in the Bronx, another really rough place. The students were impoverished, and many were homeless; it was the rare parent who would show up for parent-teacher conferences. During this time, I would get an occasional email from Bob saying the school had been on lockdown, at least once because somebody with a gun had gotten inside. He also told me that a student had bludgeoned a fellow student to death with a baseball bat.

Bob downplayed his abilities as a teacher. That was typical of Bob, but I found out later, when I met his former principal, Carmen Bardeguez-Brown, that Bob had changed lives. One Veteran's Day his students wrote tributes to him as a former Marine, telling him just that. But his being in what seemed like a war zone scared me, and by the time we agreed to get married, I went on a one-woman campaign to convince him that it was time to retire. The stress of a brutal commute from New Jersey, along with the stress of the job, was just too much. So, finally on January 30, 2014, he left The School for Excellence for the last time. Carmen wrote to him: "Your love, guidance and incredible support allowed me to do a job God knows is a challenge beyond anyone can imagine. Your faith in me sustained me when I walked through the dark valleys."

But Bob was 70; it was time.

CHAPTER 10

DIANE'S BACKSTORY

Our childhoods could not have been more different. While Bob was a California guy, moving frequently with his family, picking up artichokes fallen from a truck, I was east coast all the way, born into a stable family with a successful father, and lived in one home from the age of four until I went to college.

I was born on April 26, 1947, in Englewood, New Jersey. My parents were both born in New Jersey, but their parents were all from Italy. My mom's family came from the Piedmont region at the foot of the Alps. My father's father was born in Messina, Sicily and his mother was from Rome. The Italian roots that Bob and I had were a source of pride, and a key part of what we had in common.

In 1951, when I was four and my baby brother was less than a year old, my family moved to our home in Fort Lee, New Jersey. My parents lived there until they passed away, in 1992 for my dad and 1999 for my mom. Stability, security, and structure were built into my childhood.

My family was solidly upper middle class. My dad went to Harvard College and Columbia Law. My mom chose to stay home and take care of me. But she did have three years of college under her belt and managed the office of an executive vice president at General Motors in New York City for many years before I came along.

My family, too, was old school Italian. My dad was definitely head of the household. As the breadwinner, he called the shots. But he was a successful attorney and we never lacked anything. Even though my par-

My parents, Ed and Madeline Papalia, in my living room in NYC in 1990. They had been married for 46 years when my Dad passed away in 1992. (Photo by author.)

ents were "lapsed Catholics" I was sent to a Catholic girls' school from first grade through my sophomore year in high school. Then I transferred to the Dwight School for Girls, a private school in Englewood, for my junior and senior years.

Unlike Bob's family, both of my parents encouraged my education. They had great expectations for me and pursuing higher education was a given. That gave me the confidence to reach for the stars. In 1968 I graduated from Vassar with a degree in psychology. After graduating from Vassar, I was introduced to my husband Jon by a college friend. It was the summer of 1968, and he was working in a lab in New York, but was a medical student at the University of Birmingham in England. We had a few whirlwind dates in Manhattan, but then we went our separate ways.

He returned to his studies in England, while I went to West Virginia University to begin my graduate studies. We kept in touch periodically, but eventually we lost touch. I got my MS in Child Development and Family Relations from West Virginia in 1970, and in 1971 I earned my PhD in developmental psychology. I had just turned 24.

Following WVU I landed an assistant professorship at the University of Wisconsin-Madison, one of the premier research institutions in the country. While I was in Madison, Jon and I started corresponding again. I had broken up with someone, thought about Jon, and contacted him. We visited each other—he flew to Madison, and I flew to England—until we married in 1976.

I worked my way up to tenured Full Professor of Child and Family Studies; I was 30. My main responsibility was to teach a huge undergraduate course in child development, and then to create a new course to cover the rest of the life span. These courses typically attracted 600 or more students. No one else in the department wanted to deal with them so, since I was the new kid on the block, the assignment fell to me. Because my classes were large, publishers' reps were always hanging around, trying to land those big textbook adoptions. But one day the McGraw-Hill sales rep dropped by to tell me they were looking for a "fresh voice" to write a text on child development. He wondered if he could submit my name for consideration.

It's unusual for an assistant professor to write a textbook. The usual route for an assistant professor to take was to concentrate on research, because that was the way to get tenure. But my father encouraged me to write the book, so in 1975 *A Child's World* was published. The book was a smash, selling over 100,000 copies. Next I was offered a contract to write a second book, *Human Development*, published in 1978, and now in its 14th edition.

In 1980, when Jon completed fellowships in pediatric immunology and oncology in Madison, he took an assistant professorship in Pediatrics at Stanford Children's Hospital so I took a two-year leave of absence from Madison, and we moved to Northern California. While there, I completed the first draft of my textbook *Psychology*, along with my coauthor, Sally Olds. However, I couldn't find a university job in California, so we moved back to Madison where Jon accepted a position as Assistant Professor of Pediatrics in the fall of 1982.

In 1986 we adopted our eight-week-old daughter Anna, born in Santiago, Chile. Once all the papers were finalized, Jon flew to Chile to bring Anna home. In 1987 Anna and her father became American citizens in the same naturalization ceremony at a Madison courthouse.

My marriage eventually foundered, finally ending after 22 years in 1999. My mother passed away in 1999, one day after my 52nd birthday. In mid-March, the day after my divorce hearing, she fell and broke her hip, and despite intensive rehabilitation therapy, she did not recover.

I decided to use some of my inheritance from my mother to travel with Anna. That summer, we took a

Celebrity line cruise to Bermuda. We enjoyed the entertainment, the non-stop meals and snacks, and the time to relax by the pools. But most of all, it was an opportunity for us to spend quality mother-daughter time together. It helped us cope with the changes in our lives. We spent the Christmas of 1999 in Naples, Florida, and the next Christmas, in Palm Beach.

In the spring of 2000, Anna and I flew to San Juan, Puerto Rico, where we enjoyed private guided tours of the rain forest and Old San Juan. We ate our dinners outdoors every evening where we could hear the sounds of the coqui, a small frog native to Puerto Rico. We also took several vacations at the Chatham Bars Inn on Cape Cod, and enjoyed a return trip to Bermuda, this time by plane.

In 2000 we took our first trip to Newport, Rhode Island. A friend had told me that if I liked the Cape, I'd love Newport. So I hired a car and Anna, our housemate Jeffrey, and I were entertained the entire three-and-a-half hour ride by a professional driver who told us all about the history of the town, and what to do there. We fell in love with the place, so that fall, my friend Jeffrey and I returned and I purchased a summer cottage where Anna and I spent large parts of the next three summers.

Because Anna was in high school, I still spent most of my time in Manhattan where Jeffrey and I would see as many Broadway and off-Broadway shows as possible. I loved trying out the latest restaurants, and shopping at the famous Union Square farmer's market, or the local flea markets. I spent a lot of time with a group of "unattached" girlfriends. A frequent topic of conversation among us was whether we would like to have someone special, a significant other, in our lives. I was the only one who said "No."

Until I got that letter . . .

Looking back on the events of my life, and Bob's, I realize how significant the year of 1975 was. Not only did my first book come out, but it was also when Bob started his job as Physics Editor. Was it fate that the same person, Rob Frye, who brought Bob to New York, also gave me my first publishing contract? I don't know, but the pieces were falling into place for us to meet one day.

CHAPTER 11

ONE HOUSE AND TWO HIPS

The first few months after we were engaged in October 2013 were busy. Bob still had his house in Ridgewood, New Jersey, an affluent bedroom community about 20 miles from Manhattan. He continued teaching in the Bronx so he commuted there from home every weekday. In order to avoid the morning traffic buildup on the GW Bridge, he would get up at 4:45, head out to the Bronx at around 5:30, and arrive at school by 6:15 or so. Then he would wait in his car for the school doors to open. The commute back to Ridgewood could take a couple hours if the traffic was bad. Or it was snowy. Or if there had been a pileup on the bridge. This had been Bob's schedule since 2002. The first few months after we got engaged we could see each other only on the weekends. We developed the sweet ritual of talking on the phone every night at around 5:00 when we had our cocktail hour. He loved his Balvenie and I, being a good Italian girl, opted for Pinot Grigio. We would talk for hours about anything and everything. And often we would squeeze in another phone call before we went to sleep.

We set our wedding date for October 25, 2014, but health issues that I was facing meant we had to postpone the wedding. When Bob came to see me on October 19, I was using a walker. That was the main reason—actually the only reason—that I had kept putting off seeing him. I eventually forced myself to tell him about the walker, but feared that when he actually saw me, he'd run the other way. Of course, he didn't.

I was in excruciating pain and eventually learned I needed to have both hips replaced, which I did later that year and in early 2015. We found a great surgeon and Bob rode with me to all my appointments, pushed my wheelchair around the hospital, and stayed with me in my private room at the Hospital for Special Surgery, one of the most highly regarded orthopedic hospitals in the country, located on the Upper East Side of Manhattan. I cannot imagine how I could have handled that period without him. Recovery was long and tedious. I had been in such bad shape that I actually had to learn how to walk again. I had months of PT and OT. I went from using a walker to using a cane, and eventually to walking unassisted, but still have problems with walking and balance that make me fear going out alone.

Once I convinced Bob to retire from teaching, we saw each other more often. But he still had the house in Ridgewood and he needed to check in there a couple nights a week. Once he arrived to find his house had been ransacked and jewelry and a couple guns were stolen, making it clear that he really did have to look in on the place. Owning that house was becoming a real burden. He thought maybe we would use it on weekends, but I wanted nothing to do with the place he'd once shared with his first wife. I didn't even want to see it, let alone live there, even part time.

So, Bob devoted late 2014 to getting the house ready to put on the market for the next year. It was only then that we would finally be able to live together full time. He told me later, as the condition that would eventually claim his life worsened, that he wished he had gotten rid of the place sooner, and been with me longer. I wish that, too.

CHAPTER 12

THE ACCIDENT

February 27, 2014, started out to be a pretty typical day. Bob was happily retired but spending a couple days a week at his house in Ridgewood. It was Thursday and he was scheduled to start physical therapy for carpal tunnel syndrome at a new office in Paramus, New Jersey. But that day, a mere four months after our getting engaged, I received an email from him that said, "Tried to call you but can't get service. Am in the emergency room at Valley Hospital and am ok. Was hit by a car as I was walking into the building for PT. Getting x-rays soon. Will call when I can."

Little did we know that that accident would set in motion a cascade of events that doctors believe played a major part in triggering the condition that eventually ended his life. The police report stated, "Vehicle was attempting to pull into a parking spot . . . Driver stated that he pressed on both the brake and gas pedal while pulling in. Vehicle went up on the curve, struck a pedestrian who was walking on sidewalk and then struck the support pole for the awning . . . " The pedestrian was, of course, Bob, and had the timing been slightly different, his legs would have been crushed. Or he might have been killed. Later we found out the driver was almost 85 years old and was using his cane to press the brake and gas pedals.

Bob was released from the ER and came home to me in New York. Recovery was not smooth. Bob belonged to the Walwick Pistol and Rifle Club in New Jersey. He liked to go there on Saturday mornings and shoot some targets, and then shoot the breeze with a group of guys who also enjoyed the sport. He noticed after the accident that he had trouble holding and loading his gun. He then noticed a gradual loss of feeling in his hands, accompanied by an increase in pain. It became more difficult to do everyday things like using utensils, buttoning buttons, zipping zippers, typing, and the like. A barrage of tests (EMG, MRI, CAT scans) ensued and steroid injections and PT followed, largely to no avail. His quality of life had clearly been compromised.

Eventually surgery was necessary and on January 19, 2015, right between my two hip replacements (and while we were wedding planning!) he had a risky surgical procedure to relieve the pressure on his neck. The surgeon told us there was significant nerve compression due to the "blunt force trauma" from the accident but that the surgery was a success. Bob spent only a few days in Englewood Hospital in New Jersey before he came home. As it turns out, he was released too soon. In the middle of the first night he was back home, he experienced "a full body seizure." Simply put, he was unable to move. So, I called 911, and the emergency technicians arrived and took him to the nearest ER where he was loaded up with morphine and eventually sent home. Still, even after surgery and PT, the symptoms persisted and we knew more investigations were in order. But we made it through 2015 to enjoy our beautiful wedding.

However, that sense of relative calm was not destined to last, as we found in early 2016.

CHAPTER 13

WEDDING PLANS

My second hip replacement took place on February 11, 2015. My surgeon thought I'd be able to walk down the aisle later that year, so we set the date again, this time for Saturday, September 26, 2015. Since I was recuperating from my surgeries, Bob had to check out some possible venues for our big day. He was up for the challenge. So I sent in a Marine.

But first we considered a small, intimate celebration at our apartment. We soon realized we could barely squeeze 25 people in there, and we wanted to invite many more, so we needed a different plan.

Next, we thought a yacht cruise on the Hudson might be different and fun. There were plenty of yachts to choose from, so Bob went to take a look at a popular one. He found the boat to be small and rusty. He said if he'd booked it, I probably would have left him at the altar. So that was out.

He then went to look at Alger House on Downing Street in Greenwich Village. It is a beautiful, popular wedding venue. But Bob thought the place was too hard to find, had too many stairs, and only one bathroom. Not the best choice for a bunch of 60- and 70-year-old partygoers. So, that was out, too.

We then decided to kick it up a notch and start considering hotels. That's when we realized what we really wanted was a glamorous wedding at a beautiful hotel on a Saturday night in The Big Apple. So Bob went on the hunt again. He tried The Carlyle, a luxe hotel on the Upper East Side, but didn't care for the layout. We contacted The St. Regis, but the cost there was staggering. I mentioned our dilemma to my brother, Ed, who said that he and my sister-in-law, Taffy, loved the Hotel Plaza Athénée on East 64th Street, between Madison and Park Avenues, right near Central Park. They often stayed there when they came into the city from their home in New Jersey. The hotel is a discrete boutique hotel, part of the Leading Hotels of the World group, and related to the Hôtel Plaza Athéné in Paris. My brother remembered seeing Paul Newman in the lobby. Elizabeth Taylor and Princess Di liked it, too. So, why wouldn't we? Bob went for a look. He took pictures for me, and described the layout. We could have our ceremony upstairs in the Trianon Room and then move downstairs for the reception and dinner. So we booked it, and when the time came, ended up staying for four nights. Actually, we could have stayed forever.

Once the venue was confirmed, we needed to pick out floral arrangements, design invitations, find a photographer, and figure out what to wear. Bob went over to Brooks Brothers to select his first ever tuxedo. Since it was hard for me to get around, I ordered a shale green dress from J.Crew online. Fortunately, it fit.

Since this was a Zappa wedding, music was critical. We found the Chamberlain Brass quintet for the ceremony and cocktail hour and the Thomas Kneeland Trio to play during dinner.

We were set to go.

CHAPTER 14

OUR WEDDING WEEKEND

On Thursday, September 24, we checked into the Hotel Plaza Athénée. It's a small Beaux-Arts style hotel with a distinctly French ambiance. Its lobby is decorated with murals, sculptures, and an antique writing desk where guests check in. We were escorted to Room 1010, an elegant suite with a huge bedroom, a living room with a dining area, two bathrooms, a kitchenette, and a minibar. Best of all there was a private balcony where we relaxed after we arrived, enjoying the bottle of Veuve Cliquot that was left for us by the hotel management. That evening Bob arranged for my daughter Anna to join us for dinner. We opted for room service because it was quick and easy. After all, we had a busy few days ahead and wanted an early night.

Our wedding weekend fell at a time when the UN General Assembly was in session, something that happens every September in New York City. The Queen of The Netherlands and the President of Brazil were staying at our hotel, so the place was crawling with security. It was like an armed camp, but that in no way interfered with our plans. The hotel staff were pros at making sure everything ran smoothly. But traffic was crazy, roads were jammed if not closed, and security was tight all over town. We had many friends flying in from all over the country, as well as Sweden and Belgium, and we were concerned about them getting into the city from Kennedy, 16 miles away. But, as luck would have it, everyone arrived on time.

On Friday night, the night before the wedding, we decided to invite family and a few very close friends to a reception in our suite. It was essentially a "rehearsal dinner" without the rehearsal. That evening I met Bob's high school friend, Bill Harris, who flew in from California. Bill was a Hollywood reporter, known for his movie reviews and his interviews of just about every Hollywood celebrity. Most recently he had been on tour with Sophia Loren. I remember loving Bill's program on Showtime, *Hollywood Close-up*, which I watched religiously many years before. And there he was in our suite! It was my introduction to what I would come to know as "Zappaworld."

We chose a menu of eight hot and cold "heavy hors d'oeuvres" with wine, champagne, beer, and sparkling water. For two hours, butlers passed the appetizers on silver trays. Bob especially liked the baby lamb chops and mini beef Wellington. I loved the tuna tartare with avocado mousse. Looking back, I smile when I think of how far Bob had come in the 29 years since he told me at breakfast that The Pierre was too rich for his blood.

The partying had officially begun!

CHAPTER 15

AT LAST

Saturday, September 26, was one of those crisp clear fall days, the reason songs are written about autumn in New York. Bob and I slept in to rest up for our big day. Then Bob went out to get breakfast at Eat Here Now, a diner not far from our hotel. There he ran into a couple of friends who'd come into town for our celebration. Bob took that chance to catch up while I stuck with my usual "breakfast" of black coffee, and had a manicure and pedicure at the hotel spa.

Around 4:00, photographer Maggie Yurachek and her assistant, Jessica Liggett, arrived. The suite was crowded as Bob, Anna, and a slew of others were there for the photo op. Maggie and Jessica worked nonstop till about 10:00 that night, and the beautiful pictures I have of that day bring me comfort today.

My daughter Anna was my only attendant. Before the ceremony, Anna and I had our make-up done. Eldo Ray Estes is a four-time Emmy winner, recommended by my friend Michael Ferreri, who was there to do my hair. Eldo told me later he didn't do weddings any more (his clients, after all, include Sharon Stone and Annette Benning) but he was intrigued by the idea of working with a 68-year-old bride! Sometimes age does work in your favor!

At about 5:30 or so, our officiant arrived. Bob and I did not belong to a church, but we found a licensed New York officiant who went over a few details of the ceremony with us. Afterwards, Bob went downstairs to greet our guests.

Just before 6:00, Mary Cawley from the hotel staff came to tell me it was time to head to the Trianon

Room for the wedding ceremony. The original plan was for my brother, Ed, to walk me down the aisle, but I was concerned that my unsteady balance after surgery might propel me head first into Bob's arms, so Bill Harris stepped in and offered to be an additional escort. So I grabbed his arm, too, and the three of us—Ed, Bill, and I—headed down the aisle to the sound of The Chamberlain Brass playing "Trumpet Voluntary." As I walked toward my husband-to-be, I was never so sure of anything in my life. Nothing about that has ever changed.

The ceremony only lasted about 10 minutes, before a packed house of about 70 guests. After the ceremony, Bob, Anna, Rob Lanni the best man, our officiant, and I went back to our suite to sign the marriage papers. Then Bob and I were left alone to have a snack and toast our new life! But we didn't want to miss the party, and we quickly went downstairs where the festivities were in full swing. The Bar Seine is a romantic setting, perfect for the hour-long reception of drinks, light hors d'oeuvres, and the beautiful music of The Chamberlain Brass quintet. The formal dinner was in Arabella, the hotel dining room with lovely Murano glass chandeliers and a blue ceiling painted with fluffy white clouds. The dinner consisted of four courses including a main course of filet mignon and halibut filet. The wedding cake, with layers of carrot and lemon poppy-seed cake, was covered with flowers. Bill Harris was our wedding emcee and had the crowd laughing, and Anna gave a beautiful impromptu toast that brought tears to my eyes.

Earlier we had been asked to provide a quotation or two for the printed menu. We chose the Chinese proverb: "An invisible thread connects those who are destined to meet, regardless of time, place and circumstance. The thread may stretch or tangle. But it will never break." And this by Arrigo Bolto: "When I saw you, I fell in love. And you smiled because you knew."

When the party ended at around 10:00, we went to our room and, in a king-size bed strewn with rose petals, made love—the first of many times as husband and wife.

* * *

This is my favorite wedding reception photo. I love the look of pure joy on my face. (Photo courtesy of Maggie Yurachek Photography.)

The next evening, Sunday, we held another reception in our suite, this one for friends visiting from out of town. I spent a lot of time that evening talking with another of Bob's high school buddies, Dick Barber, who traveled from Nevada. Dick had been the tour manager for Frank Zappa's band, the Mothers of Invention, for eight years from the late '60s and early '70s. Both Dick and Bill Harris, the Hollywood reporter, became my friends, too. The reception on Friday had been such a success that we opted to have a different selection of hot and cold hors d'oeuvres once again served butler-style on silver trays. We loved having this special time with so many people who came from a distance to celebrate with us. Some had been familiar with our story; but most were not.

CHAPTER 16

MARRIED LIFE

Although Bob and I came from different worlds, we both longed for safety and security. That, as well as unconditional love, is what we found in our marriage.

When we returned home to our apartment at The Level Club after our four-day wedding celebration in September 2015, we easily developed a rhythm to our life together. Bob liked to go out and explore the city. Central Park was near our place, and he'd often hike over there after breakfast, sitting on a bench near Strawberry Field, a landscaped area dedicated to John Lennon. There he'd watch the tourists, maps in hand. He loved to tell me when one would ask him for directions to the apartment where Lennon was murdered and he would point out The Dakota on West 72nd Street. Bob was becoming a New Yorker. Sometimes he would stop at the New York Sports Club on West 73rd Street for a workout before coming home. Bob had completed the Marine Corps and New York City Marathons when he was younger, so physical activity and fitness were important to him.

While Bob made his rounds, I would spend my time reading, chatting on the phone with friends, or shop online, play Words with Friends, or complete the *New York Times* crossword puzzles. When Bob got home, we would work on a manuscript, chat, nap, or watch TV together. And we'd try to figure out what to do about dinner. I didn't have much confidence as a cook, but Bob encouraged me, and I actually got pretty good at it. At first, we often prepared dinner together. A special favorite was to make my mom's "authentic" pasta sauce. We did it assembly-line style. We'd fill a big pot with three large cans of tomato purée. Then Bob would sauté Italian sausage and throw that in the pot. Meanwhile, I'd make the meatballs—a combination of ground beef, Parmesan cheese, a slice of bread soaked in water and then torn apart, a touch of milk, and plenty of chopped onions and garlic. Most of the time the meatballs were more like meat blobs, but it still worked. After a good three hours, the sauce was ready; the aroma and taste reminded me of my mom.

Our apartment at The Level Club. All set for Christmas brunch 2017. (Photo by author.)

Sometimes when we were making dinner, I'd ask Bob how he liked "playing house." "Babe," he would say, "We're not playing, and I've got the papers to prove it!" Yes, he called me Babe, and I loved it.

Around 6:15 in the evening, often after watching *Judge Judy* or a cooking show on television in our bedroom, we'd start the cocktail hour. I'd put out some sort of simple appetizer, often cheese and crackers, and Bob would pour the drinks. He usually opted for Scotch or a single malt; I preferred white wine. Every night while we were doing this, he would take me in his arms and say, "Never gonna let you go." Oh, how I wish that could always be so.

After cocktail hour, we'd go out into our living room, watch the news, and just talk for a couple hours. If we weren't having pasta for dinner, I would often do Tex-Mex. Bob couldn't decide if his favorite was shrimp tacos or chicken fajitas. So I'd gladly make both.

Often my daughter, Anna, would join us for dinner. She'd come over after work, plop herself down on the sofa, and tell us about her day. Bob always had good advice to give her, and I think she internalized much of it. Dinner with her was always lively, with much talk about politics and other world events.

Bob loved our home and encouraged me to channel my inner interior designer. It was fun to create a beautiful, colorful, very personal space for us. Once again, Bob's support allowed me to experiment. It was wonderful to have the freedom to try something new, like cooking or decorating, when you knew you couldn't fail.

CHAPTER 17

FRANKIE AND BOBBY

The year 2015 was a big one for Bob and for us. On August 17, 2015, six weeks before our wedding, Bob, with Bob Stannard, his coauthor had published *Frankie and Bobby: Growing Up Zappa*. He started the manuscript in 1994, just after Frank passed away. He had told me about his idea for a memoir and I saw a potential winner. When I asked him why he hadn't finished the manuscript, he told me that his first wife, Marcia, wasn't sure that anyone would be interested in their story, and she didn't want to see him fail. When Bob and I finally got together in 2013, I pushed him to write the story that only he could tell.

Bob's life was forever colored by his brother's celebrity. Whenever someone noticed Bob's last name, they would often ask, "Any relation to Frank Zappa?" It was a constant in Bob's life that Frank's name would be invoked, and that sometimes people would seek contact with Bob only in hopes they could have access to Frank. But Bob's nearest and best friends loved Bob for himself. And Bob never voiced any bitterness about being Frank's younger, less-known brother. He loved Frank, and didn't think of him as a celebrity. They were brothers.

Bob's book, *Growing Up Zappa*, describes Frankie and Bobby's shared childhood experiences. It relates original stories about Frank's childhood right up until his stint at the Garrick Theater in Greenwich Village in New York City (in a show called "Absolutely Freee") in 1967. It is, of course, a historical record of Frank's early years, but it is also a coming-of-age story of two brothers who were best friends. The book begins with the boys' early years in Baltimore, Maryland, in the 1940s and describes the many moves during their childhood as their dad pursued job "opportunities" in search of a better life for his wife and their four children, Frankie, Bobby, Carl, and Candy. What I found especially touching is how Frankie protected Bobby and how Bobby adored his older brother. In fact, Frank was more of a parent to Bob than their father was.

Bob and I had started discussing the project early in 2014. He submitted his proposal to several publishers, but their reaction was lukewarm and no offers came. So Bob, like so many authors these days, turned to self-publishing. That summer, we gathered a few people together in our place to brainstorm about how to proceed. Bob Stannard was there and suggested, wisely, to end the story in 1967 when Bob, who had been working for Frank in the Village, decided that show business wasn't for him, and headed back home to California. Stannard helped Bob polish the manuscript, but the story and the "author's voice " are all Bob. I think writing this story helped Bob cope with the enormous loss of his brother, just as writing this memoir is cathartic for me.

Once the book was published, it received many positive reviews. Bob did a number of interviews for radio and magazines and was asked to "guest lecture" for a number of university classes that focused on "the American composer, Frank Zappa." He did these via Skype. And in April 2016, Bob, Anna, her boyfriend Brandon, and I traveled to Gold Million Records in Bryn Mawr, Pennsylvania, for Bobby's book signing.

Artist Cal Schenkel, who created much of Frank's brilliant album cover art, was there, too.

Many people wanted to know more about Frank
and Bob's story, so in 2017 Bob self-published *Frankie and Bobby: The Rest of Our Story.* That book picked
up where the first left off and describes his separate
but strong adult relationship with Frank, describing

*Many Zappa fans turned out for the book signing for Bob's first book,
Frankie and Bobby: Growing Up Zappa. That book, along with the
second, Frankie and Bobby: The Rest of Our Story, fills many of
the gaps in the information about Frank Zappa's life, particularly his
childhood. Both books got excellent reviews on Amazon and elsewhere. And he dedicated them both to me! (Photo by author.)*

family dynamics, and ends with our marriage. I was Bob's coauthor but the story was, once again, all Bob's. We really enjoyed working together. He would write a chapter and then I would read and critique it. We would go back and forth in this fashion until we were satisfied a chapter was publication ready.

Bob started another writing project about his teaching experience in the Bronx, but never had the chance to complete that manuscript. I would have enjoyed sharing another writing project with him, and working together as a team.

CHAPTER 18

HANGING WITH MOON AND DWEEZIL

never met Bob's big brother Frank. He died on December 4, 1993, 20 years before Bob and I decided to marry. I still don't know much about Frank's music, but I vividly remember his political commentary on TV. If I were channel surfing and saw that he was being interviewed, I paid attention. His comments were always interesting and often controversial. I remember saying more than once to Bob "In all the times I'd watch Frank on TV, it never once occurred to me that he would end up being my brother-in-law!" Bob would just smile.

Bob was not able to see his brother just before he passed away. He went to California in September 1993 to attempt a final visit, but Frank's wife, Gail, prevented that from happening. When Bob connected with Moon and Dweezil, Frank's children, in 2016, they told him their father probably didn't even know Bob had made that trip from New Jersey to see him. But Bob always wondered why Frank, himself, hadn't tried to connect more frequently with him, or, if he did, what Gail might have told him. This was one of the biggest bits of unfinished business in Bob's life.

Because of this, connecting with Dweezil and Moon meant the world to Bob, and to me. One day in May 2016 we got a phone call from Dweezil and Megan, his wife. Dweezil was in town to do a late night TV show and they had a few hours free and wondered if they could drop by. We jumped at the chance. Bob rushed over to Fairway, a local market, to pick up lunch, and we had a long, leisurely meal together. A lot of confusion and misinformation was cleared up that day.

We saw Dweezil and Megan again when they brought Dweezil's daughters, Zola and Ceylon, and Megan's daughter, Mia, to meet us. Dweezil made linguine with a fresh tomato sauce and kale salad. Visiting together was deeply satisfying family time, something Bob had longed for. In October 2016, Bob and my daughter Anna went to Dweezil's concert at the Beacon Theater, a couple of blocks from our home. Bob said, "At times during the concert I closed my eyes and saw Frank playing. That's how good he is." When Dweezil spoke of talking with Bob, he said it was like talking with his dad.

On June 18, 2016, after four decades, Bob reconnected with Moon. She came over with a girlfriend for dinner and she affirmed everything Dweezil had told us about the long separation. Then on June 20, Bob, Anna, and I were her guests at a special showing of *Eat That Question*, a highly regarded documentary about Frank directed by Thorsten Schütte. Moon visited us several times, along with her daughter Mathilda. Moon was warm and funny and the visits were healing for everyone.

We often tried to get together with Moon and her family on other occasions, too, but they were on the west coast while we were on the east, so it was difficult to arrange. But Moon, Dweezil, and Megan shared my profound sadness about Bob's passing. I treasure the note that they sent, "May you feel surrounded by Uncle Bob's presence and love. We are holding you close in our thoughts and hoping you are doing ok. XO, Dweezil, Moon, Megan, and Mia."

Bob would have been so touched by their thought-fulness. But I have a feeling wherever he is, he knows.

CHAPTER 19

MEETING BOB'S SON AND SISTER

The musical talent in the Zappa family is mind-boggling. Bob said he was the only Zappa who didn't get the "music genes." But I've heard otherwise. The story of how Bob gave Frank his first guitar, which Bob bought for $1.50, is fairly well known, but Dick Barber, Frank's longtime tour manager, recently told me that he heard Bob play that guitar and thought Bob's potential talent was at least as great as Frank's. If Bob heard that now, he'd probably roll his eyes. But Bob often underestimated himself. He didn't know how good he was. However, in the interest of full disclosure: Bob couldn't carry a tune. He said, and I'd vouch for it, that he didn't actually sing a song, but he said a song. However, he used to love when I would sing to him.

Bob's only child is Stanley Jason Zappa. Jason lives in Oliver, a town of 4,000 people in the Okanagan Valley, a grape-growing and wine-making area in British Columbia, Canada. It's a remote place, hard to get to and hard to get out of. So the opportunities to see Jason were limited. But in the years Bob and I were together, Jason visited with us four times here in New York. These visits always meant a lot to Bob and me. I loved seeing Bob so happy that "my boy" was coming to see us, and the time we spent together was always relaxed and fun. During those visits, Jason and Bob would have breakfast together every morning. While I'm not a breakfast person, I loved hearing them catch up as they ate in the dining room. And they always made sure I had plenty of black coffee in bed, where I was watching the morning talk shows or, often, playing Words with Friends. Jason was an exceptional chef, too, and we invited him to cook as much as he liked, which turned out to be pretty much every night.

Jason plays sax and clarinet, and has completed a number of European tours. In 2017 he performed in Belgium, Switzerland, France, Italy, and elsewhere in Europe. Several years before that, he played at Zappanale, the annual festival held in Bad Doberon, Germany, to honor his uncle Frank.

The last time Jason visited was for Bob's 75th birthday on August 29, 2018. Jason was returning from a tour in Finland. We knew that visit was meaningful, but only later did we realize how meaningful. It was the last time that father and son saw each other. I hope Jason knows that Bob was very proud of him and how much Bob missed him through the years.

Bob's sister Patrice Zappa-Porter is called Candy. Her brother Carl nicknamed her that because he thought she was "sweet." Bob and Candy hadn't been in touch for a long time but, with my urging, they connected in 2015. Candy is a singer who among other venues, performed at Zappanale with Ed Palermo's Big Band in July 2019. She also published a three-volume series, *My Brother Was a Mother: A Zappa Family Album*, with wonderful family photos and stories. Candy was married to Nolan Porter, an R&B singer who had a large following, especially in England. Nolan released two albums; his best-known songs are "If I Could Only Be Sure" and "Keep on Keepin' On." He and Candy also performed in the LA area, where they lived.

Candy and Nolan visited us in September 2016. We had a wonderful, relaxed evening. Bob made linguine with clam sauce, his specialty, and we talked for hours. When Candy and I recently reminisced about that evening together, she told me that even then she was struck by Bob's balance problems. I have been in touch with Candy a lot since Bob passed. I couldn't ask for a more caring sister-in-law. Sadly, Nolan passed away in February 2021.

Nolan and Candy. (Photo courtesy of Jules Waterman.)

CHAPTER 20

PARTY TIME

Once Bob and I were finally together, we discovered that we both loved to entertain, usually at home. Neither of us had done much of that in the past, so we threw ourselves into it. We gave many casual dinner parties for friends with everyone pitching in. Sometimes we'd simply order sushi or pizza—no fuss, and lots of fun. We continued entertaining right through the last week of Bob's life.

One happy time was a visit from Jonathan Goldsmith, an old friend. He appeared in the iconic Dos Equis ads as "the most interesting man in the world." Bob met Jonathan in LA, where their sons went to the same preschool. Jonathan and his wife Barbara (who was his agent for those commercials) came to our wedding. One day he called to tell us he was filming in the city and wondered if he could drop by. Never thrown by last-minute guests, we quickly put some snacks together and had a great time catching up. Jonathan truly is an interesting man; among other charities, he is an advocate for land mine victims. Bob told me that it was Jonathan who encouraged him to contact me after our seven years apart.

Bob had a lot of friends from high school in Claremont, California. One of them had his own plane and one day announced he and some classmates were flying east. We immediately invited them for lunch, so nine of his old friends piled into our apartment and spent a fun afternoon eating, drinking, and reminiscing. Other high school friends who visited in those years were Dick Barber (Frank's tour manager) and Bill Harris (the Hollywood reporter). Another old friend who dropped by was Denny Walley, the guitarist who played with the Mothers of Invention. He met the Zappas when his family moved to Lancaster, California in 1955. He and his wife Janet flew in from Atlanta to join me at a memorial I had for Bob six months after he passed away.

I was intrigued with how Bob, with so many changes of schools, had maintained so many friendships, often for decades. Bob always used to say, "To have a friend, you have to be a friend." I think his outgoing personality, modesty (he was never "full of himself"), and his sense of humor were among his qualities that drew many people to him.

Bob was also in touch with Dr. Karl Kohn, a music professor at Pomona College. Dr. Kohn had allowed Frank to audit his music composition course at Pomona. When he and his wife, Margaret, were in New York a few years back, they joined us for dinner. Dr. Kohn told us about how Frank would hand in his compositions in India ink. He remembered Frank as being very polite, respectful, even reticent—yet confident in his work. Later, when Frank became famous, the Kohns were guests at one of his concerts.

We also loved to give more formally organized parties. For my 70th birthday in 2017, we went back to the Plaza Athénée for a celebration dinner for about 40 friends. One of my fondest memories of that night was Ed Palermo playing "Misty" on his sax. And for Bob's 75th birthday, we had a catered party at home for about 30 guests.

We also had parties at home in 2015 and 2017 to mark the publication of the two Frankie and Bobby books that Bob had written. Ed Palermo played the piano at the second party and asked me to choose a song. I asked him to play the classic, "I Could Write a Book," and from across the room I sang to my husband:

And the simple secret of the plot
Is just to tell them that I love you a lot
Then the world discovers as my book ends
How to make two lovers of friends

CHAPTER 21

AN EVENING WITH "DOC MARTIN"

As we settled into married life, we also settled into some serious movie and TV watching, especially because we were pretty much homebound for the last year or so of Bob's life.

Bob was a good sport about watching the romantic comedies that I enjoyed. He sat through, and liked (or acted like he liked) movies like *Falling in Love* with Meryl Streep and Robert DeNiro, and *You've Got Mail* with Tom Hanks and Meg Ryan. Bob's taste ran more toward action/adventure and films with "Italian themes" like *The Godfather*. I don't care for films that promote negative stereotypes of Italian-Americans. *Moonstruck* with Cher and Nicholas Cage is more my speed.

We also discovered that we both liked to watch Samantha Bee, Rachel Maddow, John Oliver, and Stephen Colbert. But sometimes when "news" shows got to be too much, we'd switch to *The Big Bang Theory* and its spin-off, *Young Sheldon*. And on the weekends we'd frequently binge-watch cooking shows, especially anything with Lidia Bastianich. But our favorite series, by far, was *Doc Martin*, starring the renowned British actor, Martin Clunes.

Doc Martin is a British drama about a gifted London surgeon, Dr. Martin Ellingham, who develops a blood phobia and can no longer operate. He moves to the sleepy fishing village of Portwenn in Cornwall to become the community's general practitioner. He's a great doctor, but his abrasive manner alienates many of the locals. This is how we came to have "The Doc" over for dinner.

Through a series of events, Bob found out Martin is a Frank Zappa fan from way back. Bob contacted a friend in London to see if he could track down the name of Martin's agent. Bob wrote the agent, explaining he was Frank Zappa's brother, and that he wanted to tell Martin how much we enjoyed his show. After Bob wrote, Martin replied the next morning, telling Bob he had seen Frank perform a couple of times. They struck up a lively correspondence, starting in March 2016, often mentioning that they would love to meet in person should they ever be in the same place at the same time.

In addition to the show *Doc Martin*, Martin filmed a number of documentaries. We enjoyed *Islands of Australia* and were delighted when he told Bob he was filming *Islands of America*. That documentary covered 10,000 miles of the United States from west to east including Hawaii, Puerto Rico, and Islands off the coast of the Carolinas and Georgia, and, of course, Manhattan. A few days before filming was scheduled in New York, Martin emailed to tell us that he would be in town for one night, Thursday, August 23, and asked whether he could drop by. We jumped at the chance. When he walked down the hall to our apartment, he was carrying a bouquet of lilies and eucalyptus. I blurted out, "I feel like I know you!" He came in, and after helping me arrange the flowers, we started with drinks all around—white wine for me, Macallans single malt for Martin, Peroni for Bob—and then enjoyed a sushi dinner. We really didn't know what to expect, but in getting to know him we discovered a delightful, modest, funny, interesting guy. He told us about some of his charitable work, including Buckham Fair, held on his property in Dorset to raise funds for a cancer hospital there. When he left, he invited us to come and visit in England. But that wasn't to be.

Sadly, the next time I was in touch with Martin was when I wrote him that Bob had passed away a mere three and a half months after we had met. He wrote ". . . My thoughts are with you. I'm so glad we finally got to meet up. . . I'm really going to miss sharing what we came to know as Bobby's nonsense in his emails . . . Please stay in touch and know that there is a sad heart here in the Dorset countryside." We do keep in touch and his invitation to me to stay with him and his wife Philippa Braithwaite is still open.

CHAPTER 22

THE SEARCH FOR A DIAGNOSIS

Shortly before our wedding, Bob had had surgery to address the physical difficulties and symptoms that followed his car accident. That surgery did not improve his symptoms, and in fact his physical difficulties were becoming worse. He would tell me his hands felt like he was wearing boxing gloves. He was having greater difficulty doing simple things like picking up an object like a fork or spoon. He would repeatedly attempt to grasp it but it usually took several tries. I remember his frustration when he wasn't able to open a wine bottle. He became upset, saying, "Now I can't even get my wife a glass of wine!"

We knew these problems needed to be addressed. First, Bob went to a hand therapist who worked on his fine motor skills to grasp small objects. But that didn't really help. He tried acupuncture and herbal medicine. These didn't help either. Massage felt good, but it wasn't the solution. Steroid injections did little. It was clear that he needed more, much more.

So Bob found a neurologist who ran him through a battery of tests, including an EMG, MRI, CAT scan, a spinal tap, innumerable blood tests, and eventually a nerve biopsy. Many of these tests were painful, but Bob was a trooper and endured them with little complaint. Based on the results, his doctor diagnosed chronic inflammatory demyelenating polyneuropathy (CIDP). CIDP is a rare progressive autoimmune disease that affects the nerves in the arms and legs and causes weakness, tingling, and numbness in the arms, legs, hands, and feet. It also causes fatigue and difficulty with balance and walking, exactly describing Bob's symptoms. Bob often said that he felt like he was walking on bubble wrap.

The gold standard for treatment of CIDP was with intravenous immunoglobulin (IVIG) infusions. So Bob began these early in 2016. They consisted of three consecutive days of eight hours of infusions every four weeks. It was a grueling schedule and he'd always come home exhausted. In the midst of the IVIG infusions, Bob also went to a hand surgeon who said he needed carpal tunnel surgery, first on his right hand and later, on his left. The first operation was scheduled for July 25, 2017. The orthopedic surgeon explained that Bob would have 80% of normal functioning within three months. It sounded so promising. But that didn't happen, so the second surgery never took place. We figured out later that the carpal tunnel symptoms may have been an early sign of his disease, since in 2014 he had already undergone carpal tunnel surgery, shortly after the car accident.

The IVIG infusions lasted for two years, with no real improvement—and that was because Bob didn't have CIDP. We needed to continue our search for the correct diagnosis.

Bob was referred to the specialists at the world-famous Columbia Neurological Institute where he was given a blood test to determine if he might have a gene for a condition that was even more rare than CIDP. As it turns out, Bob did have that gene and was diagnosed with hereditary amyloidosis, a much more dire condition than CIDP. Amyloidosis occurs when a protein called amyloid builds up in a person's organs and tissues, resulting in symptoms much like CIDP. It also frequently affects the heart and nervous system, and can be life threatening. There is no cure for amyloidosis but drug infusions are being developed to contain or even reverse symptoms. Bob was fortunate to get into a trial for one of these drugs at Columbia. Every three weeks, starting in December 2017, he would go to Columbia for a four-hour infusion of a promising drug called Patisiran. His doctors felt he was beginning to improve. Bob never experienced a great overall improvement of his symptoms, but some days were better than others.

One thing Bob's new doctors agreed about was that the trauma from the car accident likely triggered the amyloidosis gene. If the accident hadn't occurred, it is possible that the gene would have remained dormant, or that it would have been expressed much later in Bob's life. No one knows for sure, but I do know I can't allow myself to reflect on these possibilities too often.

CHAPTER 23

IMPROVISE, ADAPT, AND OVERCOME

Once we got Bob's correct diagnosis, we needed to make changes in how we planned to live our life together. Marines are trained to "improvise, adapt, and overcome" in any situation. Put another way, "If life gives you lemons, make lemonade." Or perhaps in the case of my Italian guy, make limoncello. So we confronted our situation with clear eyes and shifted some of our hopes and dreams to more realistic ones. Despite his symptoms, through it all Bob showed the fighting spirit of a Marine.

One dream we shared was to travel, hoping to find a way to visit Italy and Sicily. But because of Bob's balance and walking issues (and a few of my own), we knew we were safest at home, especially in the last year or so of his life. The streets of New York City are hard to navigate under the best of circumstances, and falling was not an option, at least if we could help it. So, unless he had a doctor's appointment or an infusion scheduled, we were "in residence." Looking back, that time we spent together, pretty much 24 hours a day, seven days a week, was the most precious time of my life.

One thing we could still enjoy was cooking. When we first got together, we loved to share the task. But as it got more difficult for Bob, I did most of it, with him close by. When we had dinner, he would sit across from me in the dining room. As we shared a meal there, I told him more than once that I was as attracted to him as I was in 1986. Probably more so now that we were together and I had a clearer view of what this man was made of.

We also had to modify our cocktail hour a bit since Bob was only allowed one beer a night, and he preferred to savor that beer over dinner. No more Scotch. No single malt. Just one beer. I can remember only a couple of times when he had two. So now, at around 6:15, our "cocktail" hour began with a can of V-8 juice for him and white wine for me. The details may have changed, but the lively and loving conversations did not.

We still enjoyed entertaining and we had wonderful parties at home in 2018. First was one for Bob's 75th birthday, catered by What's the Kitch. A selection of "light bites" (which I came to call Zappatizers) was prepared right in our place, adding to the intimacy of the affair. It was a special night, made even better with Bob's best friend Bill Harris flying in from Hollywood, a last-minute surprise. For our third anniversary, the same caterer made a special dinner of crab cakes, Caesar salad, shrimp oreganata, and carrot cake for Bob, Anna, and me. And we all toasted to many more anniversaries to come.

It was during 2018 that Bob realized he couldn't sit at the computer long enough to complete the memoir he had begun about teaching in the Bronx. And at the same time, he was getting more and more disturbed and disgusted with the current political climate. He started most every day reading the op-eds in the *New York Times*, usually very critical of the Trump "presidency." These inspired him to post a series of "political rants" on his Facebook page that acquired an impressive following. On December 6 he posted, "Trump thinks his approval rating would be 75% if it were not for Mueller. Maybe he's on the sauce again. Or his tiny mind is rotting further. One thing he probably does know now is that he will never have a funeral . . . like the one we just saw for 41." Two days before he passed, Bob's mind, wit, and political engagement and observations were as sharp as ever.

I learned so much about my Bobby as he faced this horrible condition. I admired him for his courage. I loved him for never giving up. And I appreciated that no matter how bad and discouraged he felt, he never lost his sense of humor. He still knew how to make me laugh, even in the darkest of times.

CHAPTER 24

THE DAY
THE MUSIC DIED

The week Bob passed away started out much like any other. He had appointments lined up for checkups with his cardiologist on December 11, and his neurologist on December 12, and was hoping for encouraging news. He was in pain, but the amyloid protein in his blood was decreasing and his weight was increasing—both good signs. He was even starting to feel sensation in his fingertips. But his balance and walking were worse and he tired easily. Overall, though, he was optimistic and told me that he looked forward to doing more and more with me as we moved ahead together. We were even starting to believe that our dream trip to Italy might be a real possibility.

When Bob and I talked about his condition, he reassured me that he was going to be around for a long time and teased me that I worried too much. As he put it, "Except for the pain and my balance and walking, I feel good. I think we are finally getting on top of this thing. And I'm happy. Happier than I've ever been." Since he looked good, I gladly bought into his assessment. But, looking back, I wonder if he was just trying to protect me by minimizing how serious the situation really was.

The evening of Friday, December 7 was pretty typical. We were having our annual Christmas party the following night so, not wanting to dirty the kitchen, we ordered dinner in from a local Japanese restaurant. Bob had chicken Katsu and one last Peroni, his favorite beer. He ate well, as he did every night. I remember the conversation revolved around where we were going to fit the 30 guests who were coming to our party. We went to bed early and, as usual, we fell asleep holding hands.

At about 2:00 in the morning, I realized that Bob was no longer sleeping beside me. I figured he had gone to the bathroom and I called out to see if he was okay. Usually I was aware whenever he got up, but that night was different. It was strangely quiet and I had not heard him get out of bed. I also couldn't hear any of the usual breathing or wheezing problems and "sounds" that occurred every night. Since he didn't answer, I decided to get up to investigate. When I found him, he had collapsed on the bathroom floor. I thought maybe he had passed out or lost his balance and fallen. So I called Victor, the building superintendent, assuming he would be able to get Bob back on his feet, as he had done many times before. But when Victor came up to our apartment and tried to help Bob, he quickly realized something much more serious was going on. He told me to call 911, and they told Victor how to begin CPR.

The rest of the night was a chaotic blur. First, I called my daughter Anna who rushed over in 20 minutes or so. By then the emergency technicians and police had arrived. They tried to bring Bob back as I stood there in stunned silence. At some point, they assured me that they could do just as much for Bob there at the apartment as they could at the hospital. I was relieved about that, but still—it was too little, too late. Nothing more could be done. So they removed the ring I had put on Bob's finger that beautiful evening when we were finally married, and I placed it on my finger, right next to the rings he had given me such a brief time ago. The medical examiner was the last to arrive. He asked Anna and me to leave the room as he checked Bob over. Then he had us come back in so that we could say our good-byes.

And just like that, at 2:55 am on Saturday December 8, 2018, my dear husband, the man with the chocolate brown eyes, was gone.

Except he wasn't. At least not entirely . . .

CHAPTER 25

SIGNS FROM MY SPIRIT HUSBAND

Whenever we would talk about the inevitable, Bob was adamant about several things. First, he wanted to be cremated. Second, he did not want a funeral or any kind of formal memorial service. And, third, he absolutely, definitely, did not believe in an afterlife. "This is all there is," he would insist. "That remains to be seen," I thought.

His first afterlife visit occurred on Sunday, December 9, the day after he passed away. Anna and I had just finished eating dinner (or, more accurately, we had tried to eat dinner) when we heard an unfamiliar sound. Anna ran upstairs to see if anything was amiss; I checked downstairs. Everything was in place. We tucked this event away, not really sure what to make of it, but we both felt it might be Bob dropping by. The second event happened the following Thursday. Anna and four friends were at my house for dinner. After we finished, we all heard an unfamiliar sound, different from the one Anna and I had heard. Once again, we checked the apartment and, once again, everything was in place. By that time, we were convinced that Bob was nearby. Since that time, there have been many sounds that I believe are heavenly signs. Each one was unfamiliar and all were hard to describe. Eight people have been present and heard these so far.

But sounds were not the only type of afterlife visit. As I was writing this memoir, 124 days after Bob passed away, I had documented over 80 signs and visits. Some, like the sounds, were quite simple. Others were much more complex, requiring considerable energy to pull them off.

Touch is a frequent sign of an afterlife visit. A day or two after Bob passed away, I noticed two parallel bruises, in the middle of both arms, in spots where I could not have caused them. I like to think this was Bob giving me a final hug before leaving. On March 8, I complained to Bob that I needed more signs from him (I talk to him a lot). The next morning I found two bruises on my left thigh, right above my knee, each the size of a fingertip. Like the marks on my arms, they were painless and, I believe, Bob's way of saying hello.

I learned that creating familiar smells is also popular among visiting spirits, and Bob is no exception. I have smelled garlic, bacon, and toast. But the most dramatic was perfume. On the morning of Sunday, December 16, I was in the kitchen making coffee. When I came back to our bedroom, it was infused with the fragrance of Chance by Dior, and it lasted for a few hours. Bob had managed to select and spray the only perfume he had ever given me from among my many bottles of perfume. And when I looked at that bottle, I saw that the perfume in it had been reduced by half!

Spirits apparently love to fool with electronics, too. In our apartment, the TV turned on spontaneously, lights that were usually solid have flashed for hours, and four overhead kitchen lights have dimmed while I was, once again, making coffee. I think the most interesting example, showing not only that sprits can affect their surroundings but also that they hear what loved ones are saying, occurred on February 17, 2019. I was having a leisurely meal with our friend Tony, talking about a wide range of topics. Tony, Bob, and I all shared a profound dislike of Trump and the discussion eventually turned to him. When that happened, the brass lamp on the piano in the dining room, next to where we were sitting, turned off and then back on again! We think that was Bob participating in the conversation—or at least agreeing with our opinions. And once the caller ID on my phone registered "DI CHARLES." Bob's full name is Charles Robert and I, of course, am DI.

In addition to these, there were other signs, too. I've seen moths and birds, orbs, pennies, a feather; an "encrypted" chapter from this memoir; and contact from a friend, Barbara, whom I hadn't heard from in 60 years but woke up one morning feeling she "had to" find me. And I constantly feel his presence. But some of the most dramatic experiences I've had have been messages conveyed by psychic mediums.

Almost immediately after Bob passed, my sister-in-law Candy put me in touch with Nova Scotian medium Patty MacGillivray who, in a series of phone calls and texts, assured me that Bob was fine, happy, and watching over me always. She even said he was proud I had started to write this memoir!

CHAPTER 26

MY READING WITH THE PSYCHIC MEDIUM DREW CALI

Still, even with the assurances of the medium Patty MacGillivray that Bob was around, at six months after he passed away, I was at a low point. I had a core group of friends who had stood by me. But many people I thought would offer support had vanished. I was alone, lonely, and didn't really know where to turn. Then I remembered that a friend from college had told me about a well-regarded psychic medium, Drew Cali, founder of The Cali Center in Ramsey, New Jersey. I was dubious. But something had made me keep his contact information.

At the six-month mark after Bob's passing, I was sad, depressed, and willing to try just about anything. So I got in touch with Drew and on May 28, 2019, I had my first reading from him, using Zoom. The reading began with Drew telling me to keep my responses brief. So I stuck with "yes" or "no" when I could. After an appearance by my parents, whom Drew assured me were together, he asked, "Does the name Bob mean anything to you?" I simply said yes, not revealing who Bob was. Then the messages started. He said Bob wants you to know you were "made for each other" and that you were "his life" and "his rock." Bob also wanted to tell me that nothing had been left unsaid between us.

Drew said he felt that Bob passed suddenly and unexpectedly, which was true. He went on to tell me that Bob wanted me to know that what happened the night he passed away was exactly what was meant to happen; it was his time. I found that reassuring, as I had always wondered if I could have done more to save him. And then Bob said it was "nicer" where he was than he expected it would be, and I would like it there!

Drew captured many aspects of Bob's personality: his integrity, his sense of humor, his need for structure and order in his life, and his pride in being a Marine. Toward the end of the reading Drew asked me, "Does the name Frank mean anything?" Drew told me that Frank and Bob are together and "very interconnected." He told me that he saw that one of them "took care of" the other on earth, which of course was what Frank did for Bob. When I asked what they were doing, Drew said they were "playing music." It was interesting because of course Drew had no idea the "Frank" he channeled was Frank Zappa.

The 45 minutes were just about up. But Drew did pass along some final messages. Bob wanted me to know he's around all the time, and that he is keeping me safe. When it was my time, Bob assured me he would come for me and we would finally be together forever. Drew said the energy between Bob and me was so strong that it was easy to receive his messages.

This experience with Drew was life changing. Nothing that Drew said could be Googled or otherwise found on line. These were exactly the feelings Bob would have expressed to me in life. And it reassured me that although he isn't physically present, he is very much with me.

So, I booked a second reading with Drew.

CHAPTER 27

THE MARRIED WIDOW

My second reading with Drew took place on April 2, 2020. Since he already knew about Bob and me, this reading was more give-and-take than the first one. I was encouraged to elaborate on my responses, and even to ask questions.

My mom showed up first and said that she liked that I had been wearing her wedding ring. I had been wearing her ring, along with my grandmother's, on the ring finger of my left hand since my rings had disappeared. I went on to tell Drew what happened. On Sunday, June 9, 2019, I had a celebration of Bob's life, a party really, at our place. It started at 6:00 pm. Before it started, at about 5:45, I washed my hands, and saw that my rings were on my finger, right where they always are. At about 6:15, I was talking with Dweezil and his wife Megan, and was shocked to see that my rings had vanished. Megan mentioned that when they arrived at around 6:10 she was surprised I wasn't wearing my rings. So sometime between 5:45 and 6:10 the rings went missing. We turned the place upside down, but they were nowhere to be found.

Fast forward to six months later, December 7. I was giving our annual Christmas party. I used the same caterers that I had hired in June, but they brought a different "cater waiter." Shortly before the party began I left my bedroom to see how they were doing. But when I left the room, I spied a single shiny dime on the floor outside the bedroom door. I called out to the caterers asking if they believed in "pennies from heaven" because I just found a dime. Then I mentioned it was too bad it hadn't been my rings as they had yet to turn up. The waiter overheard and told me she was an "intuitive" (I found out later that's a type of medium) and she would find the rings; she just needed to concentrate. A few hours into the party there was a commotion in the kitchen. She had found the rings, all three nestled together, at the bottom of the ice bin in the freezer, one place no one thought to check back in June. I put the rings back on, of course—just a few hours before the first anniversary of Bob's death on December 8.

Drew told me it took an enormous amount of energy to move those rings, but by concentrating his energy Bob could do that. But why would he? I like to think when he returned the rings he was asking me to marry him all over again and by putting them back on I was telling him "yes."

Drew also told me that Bob wanted me to know that he caused the unexplained sounds I had been hearing in the apartment. I told Drew that every night at 6:25 I would hear several knocks that sounded like they came from the kitchen ceiling. Later in the reading Drew asked if I had a rocking chair because he saw one rocking, presumably caused by Bob. I had forgotten that I have one upstairs. Then I realized that chair is right above the spot in the kitchen where I hear the sounds! (Since the lockdown of the COVID pandemic, the knocks occur exactly every six hours. I think it is Bob's way of telling me that even though I'm isolated, I'm not alone.)

Drew also told me that Bob wanted to assure me that when I think I see him, I really do see him. This has happened five times so far. I've seen him on the staircase, I've seen him dashing across the living room, and I've seen him glowing at the foot of our bed. It all happens in a flash but it is real. In the middle of one night, I could actually feel him. I sensed "someone" was behind me in bed. I wasn't afraid. I felt his arm around me. We hugged a bit and we talked. I asked him what it's like where he is and he told me it's "wonderful." Being an Italian girl I wanted to know if he was eating; he said he didn't need to. And I asked if he had a body. He told me no, "it's all energy here." Finally, he reassured me he would come get me when it's my time. Then he vanished.

So, I was now my own medium and I was channeling my husband! I had become the married widow.

And that is the end of our story. At least for now . . .

REFLECTIONS ON LOVE, LOSS, AND THE AFTERLIFE

What have I learned in my decades-long journey with Bob Zappa, a journey that continues to this day?

I have learned that unconditional love is real, rare, and is a gift we gave to each other. And I have learned there are true soul mates who are so intimately connected they can extend each other's reach into the world. When I would tease Bob and ask, "Besides being Italian, what do we have in common?" he would look at me and say, in all seriousness, "We are one person." My sessions with Drew confirmed that this is true. And I learned that "love at first sight" really does happen, and is powerful. Sometimes you just know. Just like deep down we both "knew" when I got into his car for that first, fateful drive to the meeting in Princeton.

I have also learned that grief is a long and difficult process. A widowed friend described she felt a "softening" in her responses as time went on. And that is true for me, too. But some days are still, two years later, more poignant than others. Grief, after all, is love with no place to go. But it has helped to have friends who comfort me and talk with me about my memories of my life with Bob. And I enjoy the many photos I have of our time together. Talking with friends, looking at pictures of happier days, and writing this memoir have brought me peace.

And, finally, I've learned the afterlife is real. I feel Bob's presence, hear his sounds, and know he is watching over me always. I've learned we are spiritual beings having an earthly experience. And I am sure that when it is my time, Bob will come for me and bring me home.

ACKNOWLEDGMENTS

In many ways, writing this memoir has been a labor of love. But I could not have written it without the support of so many people who generously gave their time to help me create the best possible memoir. First and foremost, my daughter, Anna V. Finlay, read drafts of each chapter. Her faith in the project encouraged me to see this manuscript to the finish line. I thank you, Anna, from the bottom of my heart.

Heartfelt thanks also go out to the following people who read the entire manuscript: Harry Baer, Dick Barber, Carole Beebe, Kaanii Powell Cleaver, Ephraim Frankel, Susan Nichols, Ed Palermo, Scott Parker, Tom Rabak, Ann Rieck, Lana Rudner, Barbara Susinno, and Robert Weber.

A special shout-out to two college friends, Leela Pratt and Jane Moody, whose enthusiasm for my writings seemingly knew no bounds, and to my sister-in-law Candy Zappa-Porter, whose love and support helped me immensely in coping with the loss of her brother Bob.

Thanks, also, to Diana J. Basso, Esq. whose meticulous attention to detail helped make my contract a reality, to Karen Gulliver who edited the manuscript with great care, to Laurie Entringer for her striking cover and book design, to Julianna Scott Fein who ushered the book through the production process, and to Maria Olsen for her skill in publicizing the book.

And, finally, thank you Emily Barrosse, founder and CEO of Bold Story Press, for encouraging me to tell my story and for creating such a beautiful book.

Diane Papalia Zappa
New York, New York

You may also like to read these books by Bob Zappa:

Frankie and Bobby: Growing Up Zappa
Frankie and Bobby: The Rest of Our Story

Bold Story Press is a curated, woman-owned hybrid publishing company with a mission of publishing well-written stories by women. If your book is chosen for publication, our team of expert editors and designers will work with you to publish a professionally edited and designed book. Every woman has a story to tell. If you have written yours and want to explore publishing with Bold Story Press, contact us at https://boldstorypress.com.

BOLD STORY PRESS

The Bold Story Press logo, designed by Grace Arsenault, was inspired by the nom de plume, or pen name, a sad necessity at one time for female authors who wanted to publish. The woman's face hidden in the quill is the profile of Virginia Woolf, who, in addition to being an early feminist writer, founded and ran her own publishing company, Hogarth Press.